Three Friends

By Tony Rossetti

Illlustrated by Jeremy Tugeau

Justin, Paul, and Phil are eight years old. They have been friends for a long time. They have lived next to each other since they were babies. They are in the same third grade class. They are on the same soccer team. They are alike in lots of ways. They are different in some ways too.

"Paul," his mom called. "It's time for dinner."

"Great, my grandma is visiting us. She made my favorite dinner," Paul said. "She makes the best egg rolls."

"What are egg rolls? Are they good?" Justin asked.

Paul thought for a second, "Wait here. I have a great idea."

Two seconds later he reappeared.

"Go ask your moms if you can stay for dinner," Paul yelled.

Phil asked, "Where are the forks?"

Paul said, "No forks tonight."

He passed out chopsticks.

Paul's grandma showed them how to use chopsticks.

"Your grandma is a great teacher," Justin told Paul.

"You are right, Paul. Egg rolls and rice are good," Justin said.

"Can you come to my house for dinner next?"

"Justin, what is your mom making for dinner?" Phil and Paul asked.

"She is making tacos and rice," Justin said.

"But we had rice last night," Paul said.

"She makes a different kind of rice. Just wait and see. You will like it." Justin smiled.

Justin's mom showed the boys how to make a soft shell taco.

She helped them fold the soft shells. Justin's dad gave them some rice on the side.

"Is the rice hot or mild?" asked Paul.

"Don't worry, it is mild," Justin said.

Justin's mom asked, "Did you like the tacos and rice?"

"It was really good," Paul said. " I liked it."

Next, the boys went to Phil's house. "My dad has been cooking all day. You are going to love it!" Phil told his visitors.

"What did he make?" asked Paul.

"He made sauce and pasta," Phil informed them.

Phil's mom scooped pasta into the bowls. Then she poured sauce on top of the pasta.

His dad taught the boys how to twirl the pasta using a spoon and fork.

"This is really good. I like pasta," Justin announced.

"This has been a fun week," Justin said. "We tried new foods."

"Every dinner was really good. But I am stuffed. I can't eat anymore," Paul added.

"We are alike in lots of ways," Phil said.

"We are different in lots of ways too," Justin said.

"That why we're friends," Paul said.

"It's good to be friends!" they all agreed.